DISCOVERING
VELOCIRAPTOR

BY RACHEL GRACK

SEQU
ENCE

AMICUS | AMICUS INK

Sequence is published by Amicus and Amicus Ink

P.O. Box 1329, Mankato, MN 56002

www.amicuspublishing.us

Library of Congress Cataloging-in-Publication Data

Names: Koestler-Grack, Rachel A., 1973- author.

Title: Discovering velociraptor / by Rachel Grack.

Description: Mankato, Minnesota: Amicus, [2019] | Series: Sequence. Discovering Dinosaurs | Audience: K to grade 3. | Includes bibliographical references and index.

Identifiers: LCCN 2017038885 (print) | LCCN 2017047437 (ebook) | ISBN 9781681515212 (pdf) | ISBN 9781681514390 (library binding) | ISBN 9781681523590 (pbk.)

Subjects: LCSH: Velociraptor--Juvenile literature. | Dinosaurs--Juvenile literature.

Classification: LCC QE862.S3 (ebook) | LCC QE862.S3 K64 2019 (print) | DDC 567.912--dc23

LC record available at https://lccn.loc.gov/2017038885

Editor: Rebecca Glaser

Designer: Aubrey Harper

Photo Researcher: Holly Young

Photo Credits: Alamy/Daniel Eskridge/StockTrek Images, 4-5, MIROXXX/Panther Media GmbH, 14-15; Shutterstock/LuFeeTheBear, 18-19; Getty/Daniel Eskridge/StockTrek Images, 6-7, Chris Hellier, 10-11, Mark Hallet Paleoart, 16-17; iStock, 5, iStock/MR1805, cover, Crazytang, 20-21, Warpaintcobra, 24-25, Elenarts, 28-29; MaryEvans/Yuriy Priymak, 22-23; Shutterstock/Galyna Andrushko, 8-9; StockTrek/Mark Stevenson, 26-27; WikiCommons/OnFirstWhoIs, 12-13

Printed in China

HC 10 9 8 7 6 5 4 3 2 1

PB 10 9 8 7 6 5 4 3 2 1

TABLE OF CONTENTS

Meet the Velociraptor	5
Discovery!	8
Finding Velociraptor's Family	13
Digging Up More	17
Using Technology	22
Recent Finds	25

■ ■ ■ ■ ■

Glossary	30
Read More	31
Websites	31
Index	32

Velociraptors weren't very big, but they could run up to 40 miles (64 km) per hour.

LOADING...LOADING..LOADING..

Meet the Velociraptor

The Velociraptor roamed the Earth 75 million years ago. This meat-eating dinosaur was only about 3 feet (1 m) tall. That is about as tall as a turkey! Its long tail gave it great balance. It stretched about 7 feet (2 m) long from nose to tail.

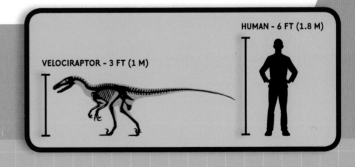

HUMAN - 6 FT (1.8 M)

VELOCIRAPTOR - 3 FT (1 M)

The Velociraptor dies out.

65 MILLION
YEARS AGO

LOADING...LOADING...

Velociraptors lived in eastern Asia. This land was mostly desert. Then, the weather began to cool. Seasons started. New plants and animals appeared. About 65 million years ago, a huge **meteorite** hit the Earth. Dinosaurs all died out. They became **extinct**.

The Velociraptor lived in desert areas in eastern Asia.

LOADING... LOADING... LOADING...

Discovery!

In 1923, a **paleontologist** named Peter Kaisen was in Mongolia. He discovered a broken skull buried in the Gobi Desert. It was a new dinosaur! He also found a large curved toe claw nearby. These were the first Velociraptor **fossils** ever found. But it didn't have a name yet.

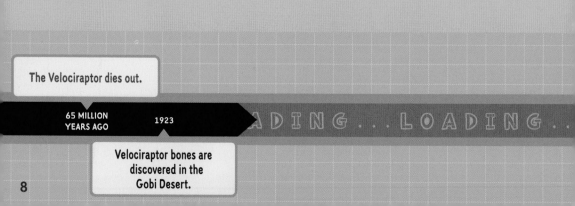

The Velociraptor dies out.

65 MILLION YEARS AGO

1923

ADING . . . LOADING . .

Velociraptor bones are discovered in the Gobi Desert.

The Gobi Desert kept the fossils in good condition for millions of years.

Paleontologists could tell that Velociraptor was fast by looking at its fossils.

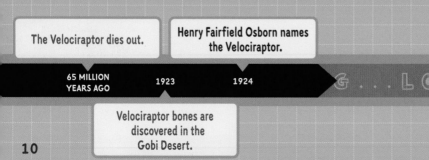

The Velociraptor dies out.

Henry Fairfield Osborn names the Velociraptor.

65 MILLION YEARS AGO   1923   1924   G...LOADING...

Velociraptor bones are discovered in the Gobi Desert.

What kind of dinosaur was it? In 1924, Henry Fairfield Osborn, a paleontologist, studied the bones. He named it Velociraptor. This means "**swift** robber." Soon, other fossils were dug up. Osborn picked a good name. Velociraptor bones were hollow and light. Velociraptors weighed only about 30 pounds (14 kg). This helped them run fast. Their teeth were jagged like a saw. Their jaws could easily snatch **prey**.

Deinonychus was discovered in North America.

The Velociraptor dies out.

Henry Fairfield Osborn names the Velociraptor.

| 65 MILLION YEARS AGO | 1923 | 1924 | 1964 |

Velociraptor bones are discovered in the Gobi Desert.

Bones of Deinonychus are discovered in Montana.

OADING . .

Finding Velociraptor's Family

At first, Velociraptors were in the wrong dino **family**! Scientists believed they were **megalosaurs**. But in 1964, fossil hunters in Montana discovered a new dinosaur. It looked like a Velociraptor, but it was much bigger. It had a curved claw, too! It was later named Deinonychus. Scientists thought it was related to Velociraptor.

LOADING...LOADING...LOADING...

Scientists put Velociraptor and Deinonychus in the same dinosaur family. They were both dromaeosaurs. These dinosaurs stood on two legs and had long tails. They had sharp claws on the second toe of each back foot. Scientists thought maybe they had feathers. They were not yet sure.

Deinonychus had long, sharp claws on its back feet, like other dromaeosaurs.

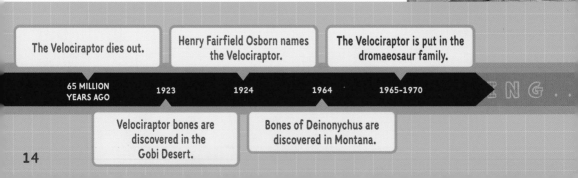

The Velociraptor dies out.

Henry Fairfield Osborn names the Velociraptor.

The Velociraptor is put in the dromaeosaur family.

65 MILLION YEARS AGO	1923	1924	1964	1965-1970

Velociraptor bones are discovered in the Gobi Desert.

Bones of Deinonychus are discovered in Montana.

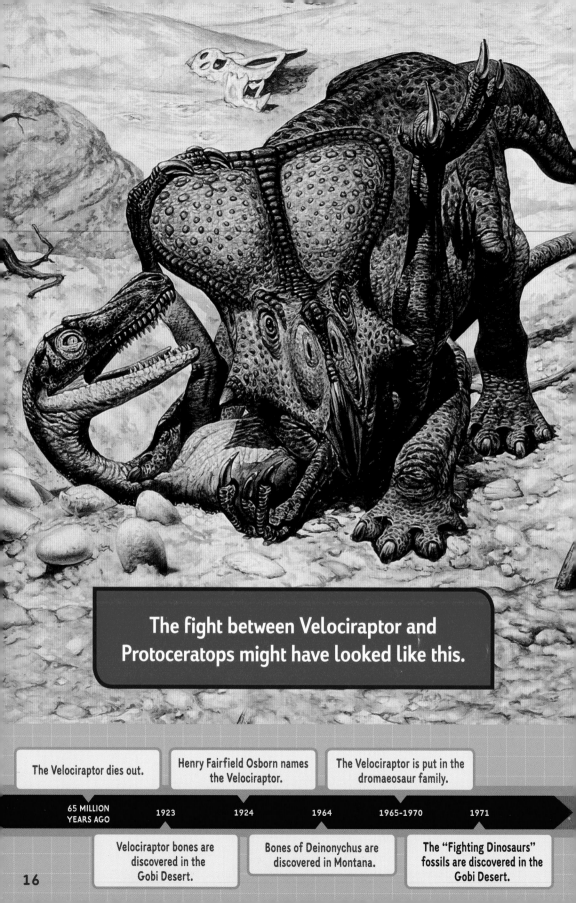

The fight between Velociraptor and Protoceratops might have looked like this.

The Velociraptor dies out.

Henry Fairfield Osborn names the Velociraptor.

The Velociraptor is put in the dromaeosaur family.

| 65 MILLION YEARS AGO | 1923 | 1924 | 1964 | 1965-1970 | 1971 |

Velociraptor bones are discovered in the Gobi Desert.

Bones of Deinonychus are discovered in Montana.

The "Fighting Dinosaurs" fossils are discovered in the Gobi Desert.

Digging Up More

In 1971, paleontologists in the Gobi Desert found fighting dinosaurs! This rare fossil showed Velociraptor in the middle of a fight. Its long claw was stuck in the neck of another dinosaur. The enemy had taken a crushing bite. The Velociraptor arm bone was still in its mouth.

Scientists dug up more fossils in Mongolia and China. In 1990, they found a few Velociraptor skeletons. They were in good shape and almost whole. One was missing its head! It might be a Velociraptor. Without the head, no one can say for sure!

Scientists used tools like these to dig out the Velociraptor fossils.

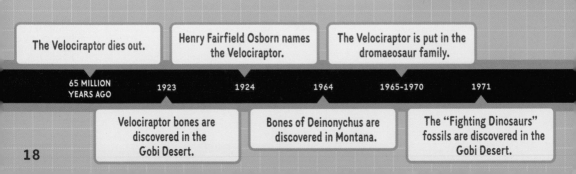

The Velociraptor dies out.	Henry Fairfield Osborn names the Velociraptor.	The Velociraptor is put in the dromaeosaur family.

65 MILLION YEARS AGO	1923	1924	1964	1965-1970	1971

	Velociraptor bones are discovered in the Gobi Desert.	Bones of Deinonychus are discovered in Montana.	The "Fighting Dinosaurs" fossils are discovered in the Gobi Desert.

Nearly full Velociraptor
skeletons are discovered.

The Velociraptor dies out.

Henry Fairfield Osborn names the Velociraptor.

The Velociraptor is put in the dromaeosaur family.

| 65 MILLION YEARS AGO | 1923 | 1924 | 1964 | 1965-1970 | 1971 |

Velociraptor bones are discovered in the Gobi Desert.

Bones of Deinonychus are discovered in Montana.

The "Fighting Dinosaurs" fossils are discovered in the Gobi Desert.

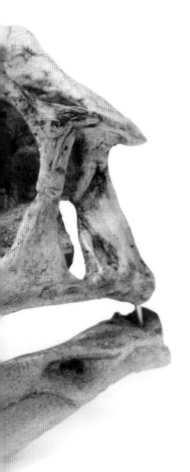

In 1999, fossil hunters found skull bones of a new Velociraptor. The jaw was not quite the same as other ones. They had discovered a new **species**! It may have lived at a different time. There were now two kinds of Velociraptors.

Both species of Velociraptor had long skulls and sharp teeth.

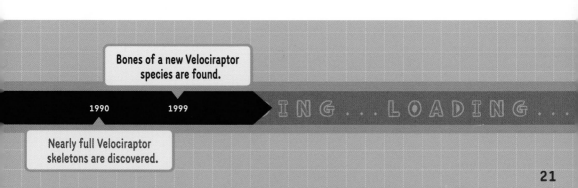

Bones of a new Velociraptor species are found.

1990   1999

ING . . . LOADING . . .

Nearly full Velociraptor skeletons are discovered.

Using Technology

For years, scientists believed a Velociraptor used its sharp claw to kill prey. In 2005, some scientists used **technology** to test this idea. They built a robot leg, foot, and toe claw. They tried the claw on pig and crocodile skins. The cuts could not kill. The claws were likely used to catch prey. Then, the Velociraptor ate it alive!

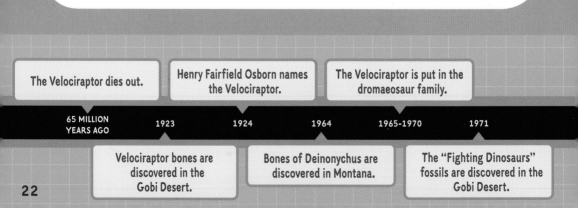

The Velociraptor dies out.

Henry Fairfield Osborn names the Velociraptor.

The Velociraptor is put in the dromaeosaur family.

| 65 MILLION YEARS AGO | 1923 | 1924 | 1964 | 1965-1970 | 1971 |

Velociraptor bones are discovered in the Gobi Desert.

Bones of Deinonychus are discovered in Montana.

The "Fighting Dinosaurs" fossils are discovered in the Gobi Desert.

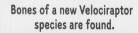

Velociraptors could use their big claws to catch prey.

Bones of a new Velociraptor species are found.

| 1990 | 1999 | 2005 |

Nearly full Velociraptor skeletons are discovered.

Scientists use a robot leg to find out how a Velociraptor killed prey.

The Velociraptor had feathers but couldn't fly.

| | 65 MILLION YEARS AGO | 1923 | 1924 | 1964 | 1965-1970 | 1971 |

The Velociraptor dies out.

Henry Fairfield Osborn names the Velociraptor.

The Velociraptor is put in the dromaeosaur family.

Velociraptor bones are discovered in the Gobi Desert.

Bones of Deinonychus are discovered in Montana.

The "Fighting Dinosaurs" fossils are discovered in the Gobi Desert.

Recent Finds

In 2007, scientists discovered a Velociraptor arm with quill knobs. These bumps are where feathers attach to the bone. Now they knew for sure. This dinosaur had feathers! But its arms were too short for flying. The feathers may have helped it stay warm.

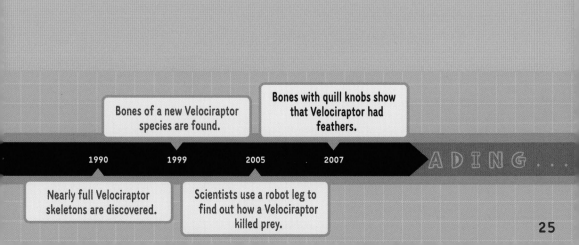

Bones of a new Velociraptor species are found.

Bones with quill knobs show that Velociraptor had feathers.

1990   1999   2005   2007

Nearly full Velociraptor skeletons are discovered.

Scientists use a robot leg to find out how a Velociraptor killed prey.

Scientists study dinosaur droppings to find out what they ate. They also look inside stomachs for food fossils. The Velociraptor ate bugs, lizards, and small animals. In 2012, paleontologists found a pterosaur bone inside one stomach. This animal was much too big to have been hunted as prey. So scientists think that Velociraptor ate other dinosaurs' leftovers.

The Velociraptor hunted small animals for food and also ate dinosaurs that had already died.

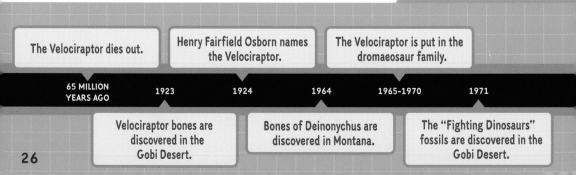

The Velociraptor dies out.

Henry Fairfield Osborn names the Velociraptor.

The Velociraptor is put in the dromaeosaur family.

| 65 MILLION YEARS AGO | 1923 | 1924 | 1964 | 1965-1970 | 1971 |

Velociraptor bones are discovered in the Gobi Desert.

Bones of Deinonychus are discovered in Montana.

The "Fighting Dinosaurs" fossils are discovered in the Gobi Desert.

Bones of a new Velociraptor species are found.

Bones with quill knobs show that Velociraptor had feathers.

1990 1999 2005 2007 2012

Nearly full Velociraptor skeletons are discovered.

Scientists use a robot leg to find out how a Velociraptor killed prey.

A pterosaur bone is found in the stomach of a Velociraptor.

The Velociraptor dies out.

Henry Fairfield Osborn names the Velociraptor.

The Velociraptor is put in the dromaeosaur family.

| 65 MILLION YEARS AGO | 1923 | 1924 | 1964 | 1965-1970 | 1971 |

Velociraptor bones are discovered in the Gobi Desert.

Bones of Deinonychus are discovered in Montana.

The "Fighting Dinosaurs" fossils are discovered in the Gobi Desert.

Most fossils are bones. They don't show skin or feathers. Then in 2015, a new fossil was discovered. It was much like a Velociraptor. The skeleton was covered in feathers! The dinosaur looked a lot like a huge bird. Most scientists now think that birds belong to the dinosaur family. What will they discover next?

Velociraptor and its relatives had feathers.

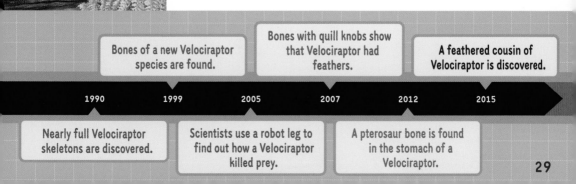

Bones of a new Velociraptor species are found.

Bones with quill knobs show that Velociraptor had feathers.

A feathered cousin of Velociraptor is discovered.

1990   1999   2005   2007   2012   2015

Nearly full Velociraptor skeletons are discovered.

Scientists use a robot leg to find out how a Velociraptor killed prey.

A pterosaur bone is found in the stomach of a Velociraptor.

GLOSSARY

extinct No longer living anywhere in the world.

family A group of related species with common features, used by scientists to classify animals.

fossil The remains of an animal or plant from millions of years ago that have turned into rock.

megalosaur A family of large, meat-eating dinosaurs.

meteorite A rock from space that hits earth.

paleontologist A scientist who studies fossils.

prey An animal that is hunted by another animal for food.

species A group for animal or plant classification. Members of the same species can mate and have young.

swift Able to move fast.

technology The use of science to do things.

READ MORE

Gray, Susan. *Velociraptor.* Mankato, Minn.: Child's World, 2015.

Raymond, Jane. *Meet Velociraptor.* New York: Cavendish Square, 2015.

Riehecky, Janet. *Velociraptor.* North Mankato, Minn.: Capstone Press, 2015.

WEBSITES

Dinosaur Days
www.dinosaurdays.com

National Geographic Kids: Velociraptor
http://kids.nationalgeographic.com/animals/velociraptor/

Your Kids Planet: Velociraptor Facts for Kids
http://yourkidsplanet.com/velociraptor-facts-kids/

INDEX

China, 18
claw, 8, 13, 14, 17, 22

Deinonychus, 13, 14
dromaeosaurs, 14

extinction, 7

family, 13, 14, 21, 29
feathers, 14, 25, 29
Fighting Dinosaurs, 17
food, 26

Gobi Desert, 8, 9, 17

jaw, 11, 21

Kaisen, Peter, 8

Mongolia, 8, 18
Montana, 13

name, 11

Osborn, Henry Fairfield, 11

prey, 11, 22, 26

robot leg, 22

size, 5, 11
skeletons, 18, 29

ABOUT THE AUTHOR

Rachel Grack has worked in children's nonfiction publishing since 1999. She holds a Bachelor of Arts degree in English, with a concentration in creative writing. Rachel lives on a small desert ranch in Arizona. She enjoys spending time with her family and barnyard of animals.